I0042585

THE STATE OF
FOOD INSECURITY IN
MAPUTO, MOZAMBIQUE

INES RAIMUNDO, JONATHAN CRUSH
AND WADE PENDLETON

SERIES EDITOR: PROF. JONATHAN CRUSH

ACKNOWLEDGEMENTS

The authors wish to thank the Canadian Government for its financial support through the UPCD Tier One Program and Bronwen Dachs and Maria Salamone for their assistance.

AFSUN

Published by the African Food Security Urban Network (AFSUN)
African Centre for Cities, University of Cape Town, Private Bag X3
Rondebosch 7701, South Africa; and Southern African Research Centre,
Queen's University, Canada
www.afsun.org

First published 2014

ISBN 978-1-920597-11-5

Cover photo by Jonathan Crush

Production by Bronwen Dachs Müller, Cape Town

Printed by MegaDigital, Cape Town

Authors

Ines Raimundo is the former Director of the Centre for Policy Analysis and Deputy Director of Post-Graduation in the Faculty of Arts and Social Sciences, Eduardo Mondlane University, Maputo.

Wade Pendleton is a senior researcher with AFSUN and directed the training of the research team in Maputo.

Jonathan Crush is Director of AFSUN, Honorary Professor at the University of Cape Town and Director of the Southern African Research Centre, Queen's University.

Previous Publications in the AFSUN Series

CONTENTS

TABLES

FIGURES

1. INTRODUCTION

Mozambique is one of Southern Africa's least-urbanized countries but, like most of Africa, it is urbanizing at a rapid rate. In 1990, only 21% of the population was living in the country's urban areas.[1] Ten years later, this had increased to 31% and to an estimated 38% in 2010. UNHABITAT predicts that the proportion of the population that is urban will rise further to 46% by 2020 and exceed 50% for the first time during the 2020s.[2] By 2030, an estimated 54% of the population is projected to be living in towns and cities. In absolute numbers, the urban population of Mozambique was 2.86 million in 1990 and is projected to increase to 16.8 million by 2030. The differential growth rates of rural and urban populations add weight to the notion of an accelerating urban transition. Between 1995 and 2010, for example, urban population growth rates were 4.5-5.0% per annum compared with rural population growth rates of just over 1%.[3]

The trajectory of urban growth in Mozambique over the last three decades is typical of the widely-observed African pattern of "secondary urbanization" (Table 1).

TABLE 1: Major Urban Centres in Mozambique, 1997–2007					
	1997		2007		% Increase
City	No.	%	No.	%	
Maputo	989,386	36.1	1,099,102	30.6	11.1
Matola	440,927	15.5	675,422	18.8	53.2
Beira	412,588	14.5	436,240	12.1	5.8
Nampula	314,965	11.1	477,900	13.3	51.7
Chimoio	177,668	6.2	238,976	6.6	34.5
Nacala	164,309	5.8	207,894	5.8	26.5
Quelimane	133,187	4.7	192,876	5.4	44.8
Tete	104,832	3.7	152,909	4.2	45.9
Xai-Xai	103,251	3.6	116,342	3.2	12.7
Total	2,841,112	100.0	3,597,661	100.0	
Source: INE (2009)					

The size of the country's older and more established urban centres such as Maputo, Beira and Xai-Xai increased by less than 15% between 1997 and 2007. By contrast, all of the others in the 10 largest urban centres grew dramatically, in most cases by over a third and some by over a half. The proportion of the total urban population in the historic centres also fell (e.g. Maputo from 36% to 31% and Beira from 14% to 12%). However, the dramatic growth after 1997 of Matola, which adjoins Maputo to the west, suggests that Maputo and Matola should be viewed demographically as the city-region of Greater Maputo (Figure 1). New arrivals from the countryside are increasingly settling in Matola and people in some of the overcrowded neighbourhoods of Maputo have relocated to Matola.[4] If Maputo and Matola are combined, the total population of the city-region increased from 1,430,313 in 1997 to 1,774,524 (or by 24% overall) in 2007.

FIGURE 1: Greater Maputo City–Region

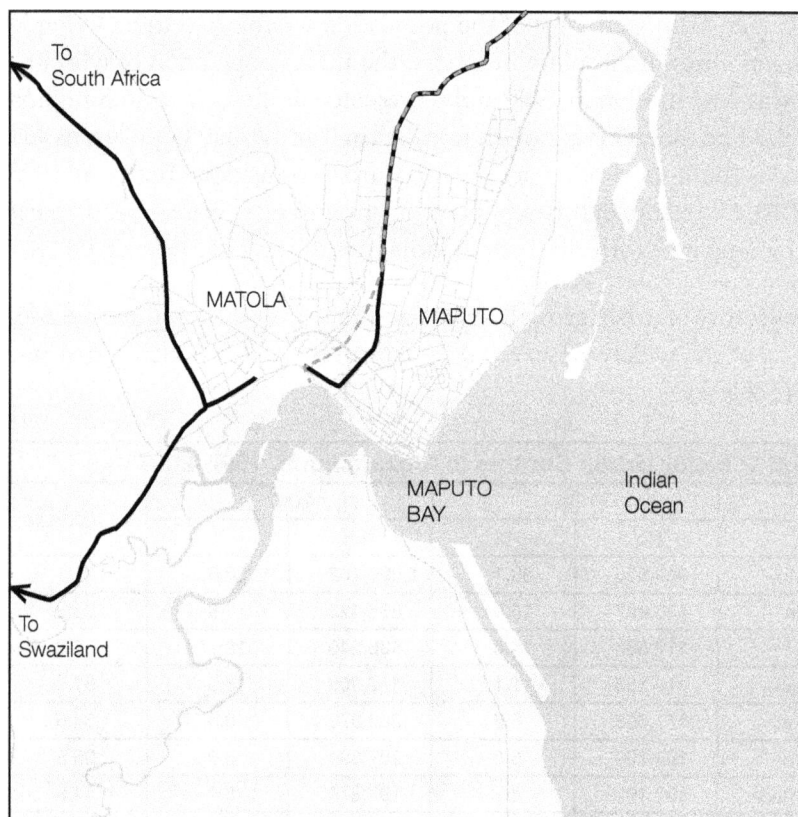

— Main roads – – – Matola/Maputo boundary

Maputo itself is the largest city, capital and administrative hub of Mozambique. It contributes 40% of national Gross Domestic Product and 70% of fiscal resources. As the World Bank notes, "there is little doubt that Maputo City has a critical role to play in the economic transformation of the country."[5] Maputo grew particularly rapidly in the 1970s and 1980s during the civil war in Mozambique after independence from Portugal (Figure 2).[6] Many displaced rural people took refuge in Maputo "creating huge unplanned settlements on the city's periphery."[7] By 1980, the population of the city of Maputo was 739,077 (Table 2). Efforts to regulate the

influx in the early 1980s by forcibly evicting people from the city were unsuccessful. The population grew by 31% in the next two decades to 966,837 in 1997. Thereafter, the rate of growth slowed but the population still exceeded one million a decade later (1,094,628 in 2007). The other fact of interest about Maputo's urbanization trajectory is its growing feminization. In 1980, males exceeded females in number but by the end of the war females were in the majority. The trend continued between 1997 and 2007 when the proportion of females increased further (Table 2).

FIGURE 2: Population of Maputo, 1940–2007

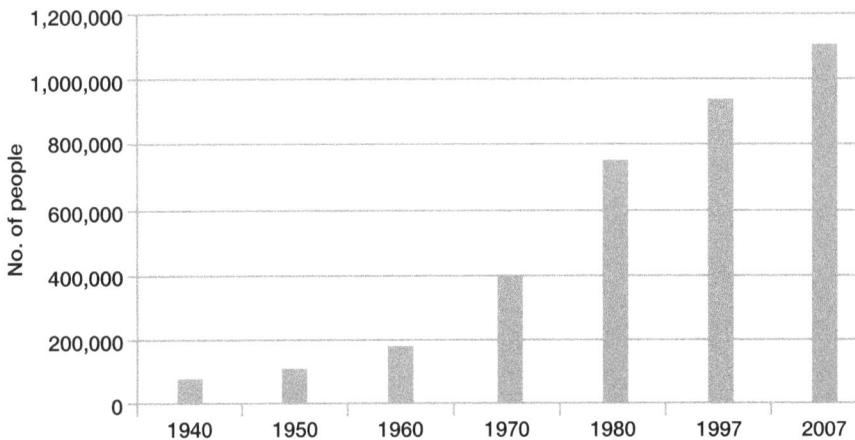

TABLE 2: Feminization of Population of Maputo, 1980–2007						
	1980		1997		2007	
	No.	%	No.	%	No.	%
Male	382,933	51.8	473,728	49.0	532,570	48.6
Female	356,144	48.2	492,109	51.0	562,058	51.4
Total	739,077	100.0	966,837	100.0	1,094,628	100.0
Source: INE (2009)						

Maputo is divided into seven municipal districts (including Kanyaka Island with a population of only 5,000 and Katembe across the bay with a population of 20,000) (Figure 3). The other five mainland districts each have a population of over 100,000. Districts are divided into *bairros* (or wards) for administrative purposes. The urban landscape is commonly divided into three areas. The first is the central nucleus of solid buildings that constitutes the wealthiest area of the city and is made up of the *bairros* of Sommerschield, Polana, Coop and Triunfo, Central, Malhangalene and Alto Maé. All are part of the Kampfumo Municipal District. Second are the poorer residential suburbs, which occupy the largest area of the city and mostly comprise buildings made of reed, wood and zinc sheeting. They cover the Municipal Districts of Nhlamankulu and Kamaxak-eni and include *bairros* such as Malanga, Chamanculo, Xipamanine, Aero-porto, Benfica, Malhazine, Hulene, Laulane, Forças Populares and 25 de Junho. Third are the peri-urban Municipal Districts of Kamavota and Kamabukwane with *bairros* such as Zimpeto, Mahotas, Magoanine and C.M.C. A recent study of Maputo suggests that its spatial structure is now fundamentally dualistic, comprising "the rich city or city of tall build-ings" (Kampfumo) and the "poverty belt" (all the other districts).[8]

FIGURE 3: Maputo Municipal Districts

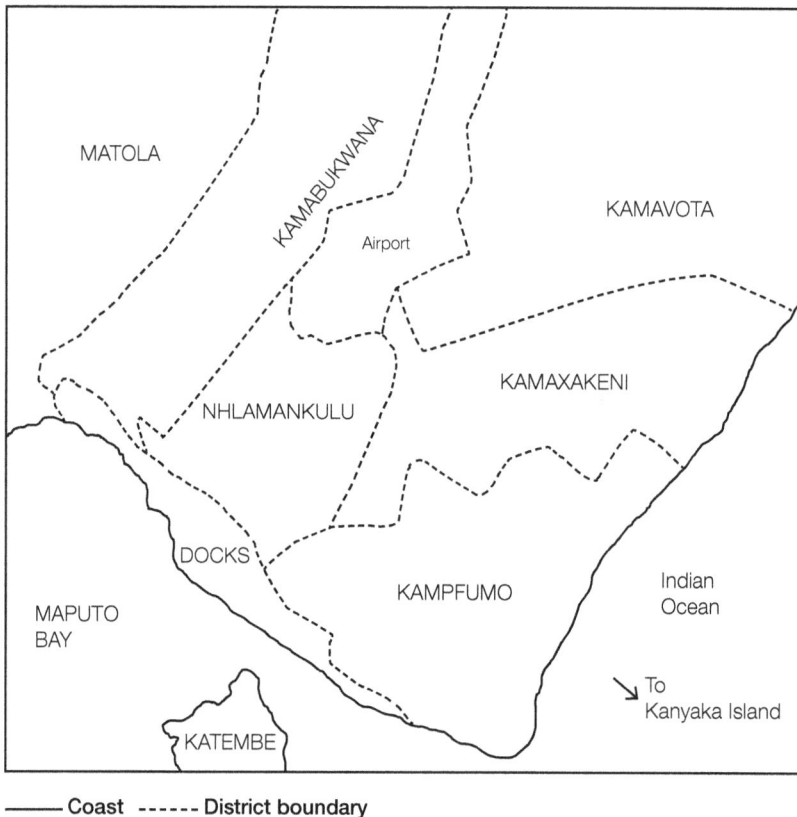

——— Coast ------ District boundary

The growth of Maputo between 1997 and 2007 was geographically uneven (Table 3). The two central municipal districts of Kampfumo and Nhlamakulu actually lost population during the decade (a decline of over 50,000 in total). The primary reason for the change in Kampfumo was a gentrification process that saw the poor areas of the district replaced by upmarket housing and the relocation of the former residents. Pockets of poverty remain and it is still possible to see "a palace standing side by side with a rudimentary shack."[9] There was a slight increase in population in Kamaxakeni Municipal District between 1997 and 2007, but most of the

growth was concentrated in the peripheral districts of Kamavota (which grew by over 60,000) and Kamabukwana (which adjoins Matola and grew by over 80,000) as a result of internal relocation and in-migration.

TABLE 3: Population Redistribution in Maputo, 1997-2007

Municipal District	1997	2007	Difference
Kampfumo	154,284	108,353	-45,931
Nhlamankulu	162,750	155,264	-7,486
Kamaxakeni	210,551	224,181	+13,640
Kamavota	228,244	289,864	+61,620
Kamabukwana	211,008	293,716	+82,708
Source: National Institute for Statistics			

The basic differences between the "rich city" and the "poverty belt" can be seen in statistics relating to service provision in the various districts (Table 4). The vast majority (over 90%) of the 27,000 housing units in the rich city are electrified, have toilets and have access to running water on-site. In the poverty belt, there are differences from district to district but, in each, 30-40% of houses do not have electricity, 70-80% do not have toilets and as many as 64% (in Kamavota) do not have water on-site. The other main difference within the poverty belt is population density with Nhlamankulu and Kamaxakeni having much higher concentrations of people than the peri-urban districts of Kamavota and Kamabukwana.

TABLE 4: Services in Municipal Districts, 2007

	Kampfumo	Nhlamankulu	Kamaxakeni	Kamavota	Kamabuk-wana
No. of Houses	26,884	30,315	41,443	56,395	57,995
Persons/sq km	8,788	19,236	18,421	2,706	5,503
% electricity	98	55	68	61	54
% toilets	93	29	19	22	24
% water	92	77	54	36	53
Source: Adapted from Barros et al., "Urban Dynamics in Maputo, Mozambique", p. 78.					

About three-quarters of Maputo's population live in informal *bairros* in the poverty belt. Although these *bairros* share certain general characteristics, including overcrowding, inadequate services and high levels of informal economic activity, they do vary in character and appearance. For example, most of the more central *bairros* are "congested and hectic, with over-populated houses, narrow alleyways and filled with small shops, markets, vendors, repair-shops, bars and other institutions" and a large number of people who rent houses or rooms to be closer to the city centre.[10] In less dense, peri-urban *bairros*, by contrast, there is less congestion, a more

orderly arrangement of housing, fewer commercial activities and people tend to leave during the day to work or seek work elsewhere. In all semi-formal and informal *bairros*, the poorest and most destitute live in rural "stick houses" or corrugated iron shacks.[11]

Households in the informal areas of the city are fluid and diverse. According to one study, residents themselves distinguish five categories of poor household, each with their own local name: (i) poor households of long-standing without the means to improve their situation; (ii) households that have become poor as a result of specific events or circumstances, including xiculungo households (usually headed by single, divorced or widowed women with no social networks or rural connections); (iii) households that are able to conserve and use what little they have to "have bread and tea every day"; (iv) households headed by single women with many children; and (v) households with a small but regular income that is still insufficient to feed everyone.[12] Many people live in large households because a separate dwelling is unaffordable.[13] Women are also taking increasing control over their own lives by forming female-headed households and establishing close female-focused social networks.[14]

Several surveys conducted in Maputo in recent years shed light on different facets of the struggle for survival in the city's informal *bairros*. These include studies of household poverty, housing and land access, water supplies, waste-picking and informal enterprises.[15] While these studies provide useful background for understanding the dynamics of poverty in Maputo, none explicitly focuses on the dimensions and determinants of food security. One exception is a study of the nutritional status of children and youth in the city published in 2003 using longitudinal anthropomorphic data from the 1990s.[16] The study collected data on over 2,000 schoolchildren and found that the primary nutritional deficiency was wasting (low weight for height) while rates of stunting (low height for age) had fallen significantly over the decade and rates of overweight had increased. Wasting and stunting were more prevalent amongst children of lower socio-economic status. The study did not relate the nutritional status of children to household characteristics and did not identify where and how children accessed food.

This AFSUN report presents the results of the first systematic survey of food security at the household level in Maputo using well-tested food security indicators for which it is much easier and less expensive to collect information. The research was conducted as part of the 11-city AFSUN baseline survey in 2008/2009. The next section of the report briefly outlines the survey methodology used. The second section examines the demographic and socio-economic characteristics of the surveyed households. The third discusses the prevalence of food insecurity and the fourth looks at the food sourcing strategies of households. The report concludes with an examination of policy responses to the crisis of food insecurity in the city and country.

2. METHODOLOGY

Many in-depth studies of poverty in Maputo focus on only a few *bairros*. The aim of the AFSUN study was to ensure broader city-wide coverage of the "poverty belt." The survey was therefore undertaken in all five municipal districts on the mainland (with Katembe and Kanhaca districts excluded). The project aimed to interview 400 households across the city. The number of households selected for interview in each district was proportional to the overall population of the district in 2007 (with the exception of Kampfumo). Given the study's focus on poverty and food insecurity, only a small number of households were surveyed in Kampfumo, in two of the district's poorer wards. Within each *bairro* in a district, the same number of households were randomly selected for interview. With minor adjustments in the field, a total of 397 questionnaires were eventually completed in 43 wards of the city: 13 in Kampfumo, 61 in Nhlamanculo, 89 in Kamaxakeni, 118 in Kamavota and 116 in Kamubukwana (Table 5).

TABLE 5: Sampling Frame by District and Ward		
Municipal Districts	Bairros (Wards)	No. of Households
Kampfumo	Alto Maé "A"	6
	Central "B"	7
	No. Surveyed	13
Nlhamanculo	Aeroporto A	6
	Aeroporto B	6
	Minkadjuíne	6
	Unidade 7	6
	Chamanculo A	6
	Chamanculo B	6
	Chamanculo C	6
	Chamanculo D	6
	Malanga	6
	Munhuana	6
	Sample size	60
	Completed	61

Table 5 continues on page 8

Municipal Districts	Bairros (Wards)	No. of Households
Kamaxakeni	Mafalala	11
	Maxaquene A	11
	Maxaquene B	11
	Maxaquene C	11
	Maxaquene D	11
	Polana Caniço A	11
	Polana Caniço B	11
	Urbanização	11
	Sample size	88
	Completed	89
Kamavota	Mavalane A	11
	Mavalane B	11
	FPLM	11
	Hulene A	11
	Hulene B	11
	Ferroviário	11
	Laulane	11
	3 de Fevereiro	11
	Mahotas	11
	Albazine	11
	Costa do Sol	11
	Sample size	122
	Completed	118
Kamubukwana	Bagamoyo	10
	George Dimitrov (Benfica)	10
	Inhagoia A	10
	Inhagoia B	10
	Jardim	10
	Luís Cabral	10
	Magoanine	10
	Malhazine	10
	Nsalane	10
	25 de Junho A	10
	25 de Junho B	10
	Zimpeto	10
	Sample size	120
	Completed	116
Total sample		400
Completed		397

3. HOUSEHOLD STRUCTURE

To explain inter-household differences in vulnerability to food insecurity in Maputo, it is necessary to look first at variations in household structure and composition. Maputo certainly has a very different household profile than the other 10 SADC cities surveyed by AFSUN. First, average household size is significantly higher in Maputo (at 6.9 persons compared with the regional average of 5.0). Two-thirds of Maputo households have more than 5 members, compared to only 28% in the region at large (Figure 4).

FIGURE 4: Size of Surveyed Households in Maputo and SADC Region

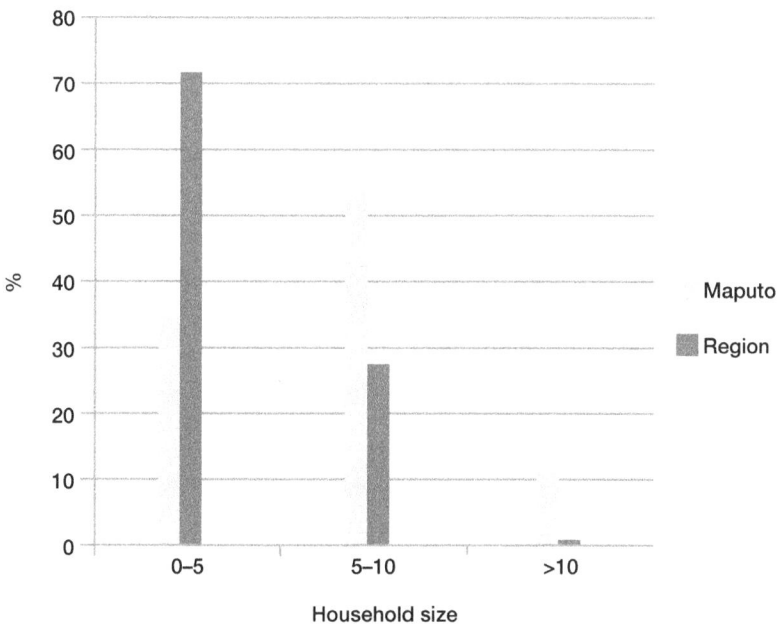

Second, and partly explaining the larger household size, there is a disproportionate number of extended households in the city. For purposes of analysis, AFSUN identifies four main types of household, based on the sex and primary relationship of the household head: (a) female-centred households (headed by a woman without a male spouse or partner); (b) male-centred households (headed by a man without a female spouse or partner); (c) nuclear households of immediate relatives (usually male-headed with a female spouse or partner) and (d) extended households of immediate and distant relatives and non-relatives (again usually male-headed with a female spouse or partner). Maputo has fewer female-centred, male-centred and nuclear households than the regional average but twice as many extended households (45% versus 22% of the total) (Table 6).

TABLE 6: Types of Surveyed Household in Maputo and Region		
	Maputo (%)	Region (%)
Female-centred	27	34
Male-centred	8	12
Nuclear	21	32
Extended	45	22
N	397	6,452

A third significant difference relates to the migration histories of household members. For example, in Maputo, only 19% of the household members were born in a rural area compared to the regional average of 35%. Sixty four percent of the surveyed population was born in Maputo compared to 44% in the region who live in their city of birth. In other words, these areas of Maputo contain fewer rural-urban migrants than equivalent neighbourhoods in all of the other cities surveyed.

Fourth, 20% of Maputo households have members working away from the city as migrants (primarily in South Africa), compared with only 8% of households in the region as a whole. Mozambique has a long history of sending migrants to South Africa to work but most have traditionally migrated from rural areas in the centre and south of the country.[17] This finding indicates that a significant minority of urban households now send members to work across the border.[18]

Maputo is similar to the regional pattern in two respects. First, the gender structure of household members in Maputo does not differ significantly from the regional average: 53% of household members in Maputo are female, compared with a regional average of 54%. Second, the age distribution of household members does not vary significantly from the regional average (Figure 5). Maputo's households are generally youthful with 72% under the age of 30 and just over a third who are 15 and younger (compared with 68% and 32% for the region as a whole). Maputo has proportionately fewer in the 30-44 age range (probably a reflection of migration) and fewer elderly people over 60. A predominantly younger population has important implications since the dependency ratio is likely to be high and the impact of food insecurity on children is likely to be greater.

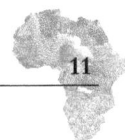

FIGURE 5: Age Distribution of Maputo and SADC Surveyed Population

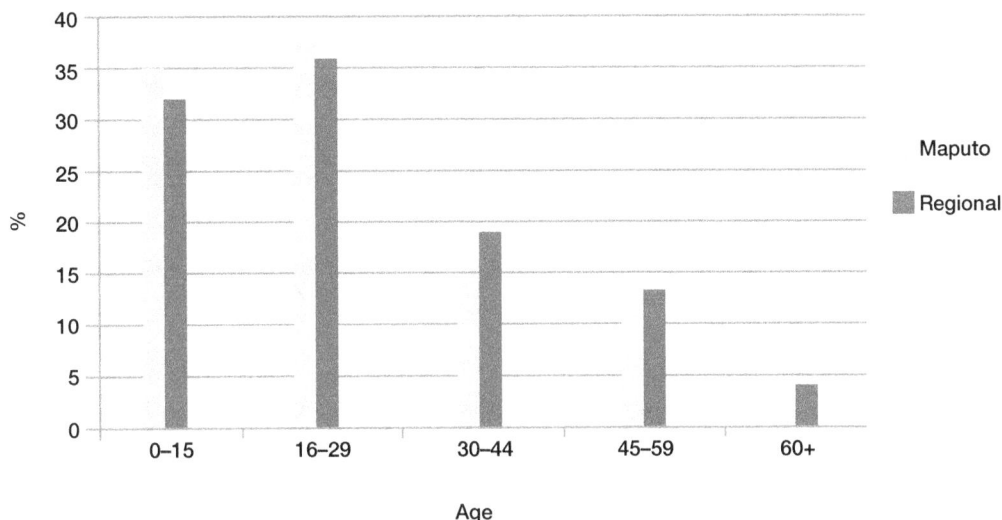

4. Maputo's Poor

Mozambique has had one of Africa's fastest growing economies over the last decade, with an annual GDP growth rate of 5-7%. However, the ravages of the civil war meant that this growth was from a very low base. The vast majority of the country's population still live in poverty. In 2008/2009, the national poverty headcount was 54.7% (up from 54.1% in 2002/2003).[19] In Maputo, by contrast, the poverty rate dropped from 53.6% to 36.7% between 2002/2003 and 2008/2009. Are Maputo's residents better or worse off than those of other cities in the region? In the 1980s and 1990s, the unequivocal answer would have been "undoubtedly worse." But with robust national economic growth over the last decade, and growing levels of formal employment, the situation has become more complicated.

A recent study based on data from the National Household Budget Survey in 2007/2008 used a variety of poverty indicators including absolute poverty (consumption poverty), non-monetary measures and anthropomorphic measurements. The authors conclude that the data "provides solid evidence of significant progress across a range of non-monetary indicators (from the previous survey in 2002/2003) at both the national and regional levels. These include large improvements in access to education (at both primary and secondary levels), improved access to health services, particularly in rural areas, increases in asset ownership by households, and improvements in housing quality."[20] At the same time, national consumption poverty (particularly food consumption) remained virtually static. However, there were significant regional variations, with some areas becoming more and some less consumption poor. In the urban South (which includes Maputo) there was a 10% decline in consumption poverty. At the same time, inequality increased. In 2002/2003, for example, the highest income quintile spent 16% of their income on food while the lowest quintile spent 43%. In 2008/2009, the equivalent figures were 18% and 48%.

The AFSUN baseline survey provides a more detailed picture of household poverty in the poverty belt of Maputo. However, different measures of poverty were used including household income, food expenditure and the Lived Poverty Index (LPI). The reported median household income for the month prior to the survey was MZN3,000 (USD125).[21] This means that half the households had monthly incomes of less than USD125 or about USD4.20 per day. Based on a mean household size of 7, that works out to be less than USD0.60/person/day. About 10% of households reported no income at all. The regional average for the proportion of household expenditure on food was 50%. Maputo is close to this figure (at 53%). Of the 11 cities surveyed, only Harare, Lusaka and Cape Town had higher food expenditure scores.

The third measure, the LPI, was used to capture the subjective experience of poverty.[22] Maputo had a mean LPI of 1.1, which is close to the regional average of 1.2. The Maputo LPI was the same as Windhoek and Gaborone (Figure 6) and lower (better) than Harare, Lusaka, Maseru and Manzini.

FIGURE 6: Comparative Lived Poverty Index Scores

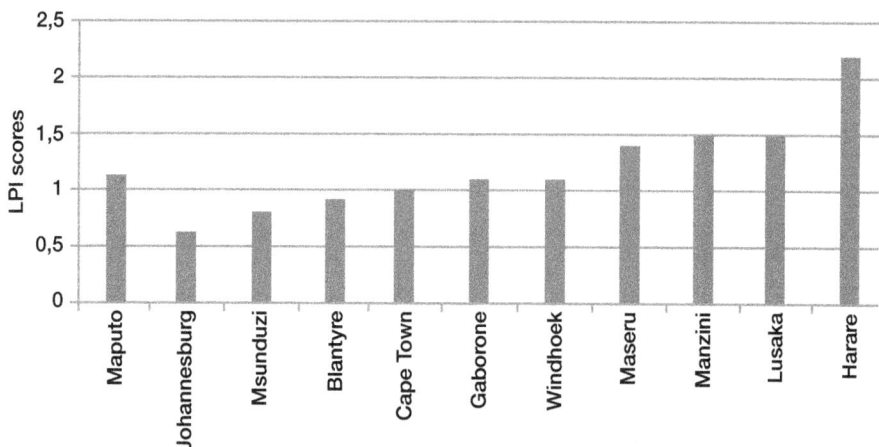

The three South African cities and Blantyre scored lower than Maputo. What this suggests is that the residents of the poorer *bairros* of Maputo experience high levels of lived poverty but they are equal to or better off

than the residents of most SADC cities outside South Africa. However, there was a notable difference within the Maputo sample between those living in informal shelters and formal housing. Seventeen percent of those in informal housing had scores above 2.0, compared with only 4% of those in formal housing. Or again, 35% of those in informal housing had scores of less than 1.0 compared with 58% of those in formal housing.

One of the reasons for the fall in poverty levels in Maputo after 2000 was an increase in formal employment opportunities. The National Household Budget Survey found that this was most significant at the lower end of the labour market. For example, there was a slight increase in formal employment (50% to 53%) and decline in informal employment (49% to 43%) in the highest income quintile in the city (Table 7). In the lowest income quintile, there was a far more dramatic shift, with the formal employment rate rising from 15% to 39% and the informal dropping from 85% to 57%. The AFSUN survey found that in the surveyed areas, full-time employment was 43% and part-time/casual employment was 17% (Table 8).

TABLE 7: Formal and Informal Employment in Maputo, 2002–2009				
	Formal Employment (%)		Informal Employment (%)	
	2002/2003	2008/2009	2002/2003	2008/2009
Highest quintile	50	53	49	43
Lowest quintile	15	39	85	57
Source: Adapted from Paulo et al (2011: 17)				

TABLE 8: Employment Status of Surveyed Household Members		
	No.	%
Working full-time	633	43.4
Working part-time/casual	249	17.0
Working – status unknown	19	1.3
Not working – looking for work	167	11.4
Not working – not looking for work	394	26.9
	1,462	100.0

Since the line between formal and informal employment is somewhat blurred in Mozambique and would not always be obvious to employees, the AFSUN survey employment figures for both full-time and part-time jobs probably include people working for both formal and informal employers. In terms of the occupational breakdown, 38% were in semi-skilled and unskilled jobs (with services and domestic work most important), 34% were in more skilled jobs and the rest were working in the informal economy (Table 9).

Despite the fact that only 46% of the surveyed population were working full-time, two-thirds of the households reported that they had earned wage income in the month prior to the survey. The discrepancy is because many households also contain unemployed adults. The second most important income source (for 25% of households) was self-employment in the informal economy. Other sources of income for a minority of households include casual work (14% of households), rental income (10%), sale of agricultural produce (10%) and social grants (7%). Surprisingly, given that 20% of households have an absent migrant, only 5% received cash remittances in the month prior to the survey. This may simply reflect the remitting patterns of migrants, who do not always remit on a monthly basis. The other notable characteristic of household income strategy is diversification. The mean household income in the month prior to the survey was MZN4,667 and is made up of multiple income streams. Over 70% of households have more than one stream. Of these 28% have two, 21% have three, 13% have four and 11% have five or more.

TABLE 9: Occupations of Surveyed Household Members		
	No.	%
Unskilled/ Semi-skilled		38.2
Service worker	109	12.9
Domestic worker	60	7.0
Farmer	47	5.5
Security personnel	44	5.2
Truck driver	24	2.8
Mine worker	16	1.8
Agricultural worker	11	1.9
Police/ Military	9	1.1
Skilled		34.3
Professional	106	12.5
Civil servant	70	8.2
Supervisor	42	5.0
Skilled manual worker	19	2.2
Teacher	19	2.2
Businessperson	10	1.2
Health worker	10	1.2
Employer/ Manager	9	1.1
Office worker	6	0.7
Informal economy		27.9
Trader/ hawker/ vendor	229	27.0
Informal sector producer	8	0.9
Total	848	

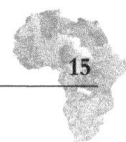

Wage employment was the largest contributor to household income over-all (averaging MZN4,172) and constituting 64% of total income earned by all households combined (Table 10). The average income from infor-mal economy activity, the second most important income source, was much lower (at MZN2,320) and only 14% of total income earned by all households combined. While formal business ownership was the most lucrative activity, only 4% of households earned income in this manner. Casual work contributed just 6% of total income of all household com-bined and remittances only 2% (about the same as rental income). Income from the sale of rural and urban home-grown produce is only garnered by a small minority of households (less than 10%) and the amount earned is only around 2% of total income for all households combined. Although wages are generally low in Maputo, it is clear that access to wage income is pivotal for households to climb out of poverty and food insecurity.

TABLE 10: Household Income Sources

	No. of Households	% of Households	Mean Income in Prior Month (MZN)	Share of Income of All Households Combined (%)
Employment	263	66.2	4,172	64.4
Informal business	101	25.4	2,320	13.8
Casual work	56	14.1	1,717	5.6
Rental income	38	9.6	1,132	2.5
Social grants/pensions	27	6.8	2,582	4.1
Sale of rural farm products	22	5.5	1,089	1.4
Sale of urban farm products	21	5.3	617	0.8
Cash remittances	21	5.3	1,920	2.4
Formal business	15	3.8	5,570	4.9
Income from gifts	3	0.8	488	0.1
Income from aid	2	0.5	450	0.1
Average household income			4,667	

A quarter of the households surveyed obtained income through participa-tion in Maputo's thriving and highly-competitive informal economy.[23] This is well above the regional average of 15%. Only Blantyre (44%), Harare (42%) and Lusaka (28%) had higher levels of participation. In most of the other cities surveyed less than 10% of the households derive income from informal activity.[24] A recent description of informality in Maputo captures elements of the character and dynamism of the sector:

> Street commerce has burgeoned all over the city. Dumba-nengues (concen-trations of informal traders) mushroomed, and some grew to engulf entire neighbourhoods. This proliferation has all but choked the more tradition-

al forms of small-scale commerce – by the turn of the century, many of Maputo's formal marketplaces lay dormant, surrounded by the swarming hives of street commerce. In the process of growth, some of the street commerce has become stationary and formalized through the city's attempts to tax and regulate it; much of it, however, has remained mobile, affording an easy point of entry into the urban economy for workers with the lowest level of financial and human capital. Hence, despite the status and income disadvantage of street commerce relative to other forms of urban employment, this sector itself is internally stratified, with stationary commerce (in makeshift kiosks or stands) commanding higher prestige and income than mobile vending. [25]

Conventionally, women have dominated the informal economy but unemployed men have a growing presence, although they tend to view participation as a "stop-gap" on the road to wage employment. The municipality recognizes four different classes of marketplace. Class A and B markets are provided with infrastructure (including toilets and drainage) while Class C markets are not. Class D markets are more informal and are not acknowledged as such. In 2008/2009, when this study was conducted, there were 6 Class A, 7 Class B, 27 Class C and 23 Class D markets in Maputo. [26] Until recently, Xikhelene was a typical Class D market with several thousand static and mobile vendors selling a wide variety of goods and services including fruit, vegetables, fish, meat, live poultry, cellphone services, new and second-hand clothes, groceries, sweets, spices, soft drinks, alcoholic drinks, traditional medicine, equipment and cosmetics. [27] Vendors obtain their supplies direct from the countryside or from other markets (such as the wholesale market in Zimpeto) or from shops and supermarkets, where they try to buy in bulk and sell in smaller units. Every day trucks arrive at the market with goods in large quantities (frozen fish from Angola, bread from local bakeries and fruit from South Africa) to sell to the vendors. [28] In 2009, under the World Bank-funded ProMaputo upgrading project, two-thirds of the market was demolished to make way for a new transportation hub, causing considerable hardship and financial loss for the vendors. [29]

The informal food economy is not confined to the markets and is particularly visible and extensive on the streets and in the *bairros* of Maputo. Tens of thousands of street vendors sell a range of fresh and processed food, often from the same stall. Most of the fresh fruit and vegetables and processed food (such as sweets and chips) are imported from South Africa. Within the *bairros*, many individual dwellings have small backyard stalls selling the same items in smaller quantities. A recent study of the central Mafalala *bairro* shows that the purpose of these stalls (*bancas*) is not simply to generate income through food re-sale but to supplement the quantity

and quality of food available to the household.[30] The household eats from food purchased from the *banca* and sells its leftovers through the *banca*. Outside schools, where children do not receive any sustenance during the day, informal vendors sell food in small, affordable quantities. The absence of fresh produce is notable at these stalls, which primarily sell processed "junk food" including crisps, biscuits and sweets. Many of the backyard and school *bancas* are actually managed by children themselves.

5. Sources of Food

In many of the cities in the region, supermarkets are rapidly growing in importance as a source of basic foodstuffs for the urban poor.[31] Across the region as a whole, 79% of poor urban households normally source some of their food from supermarkets (though only 5% do so on a daily basis). In South African cities such as Cape Town, Johannesburg and Msunduzi, the figure is over 90%. The picture in Maputo is very different (Table 11).[32] The number of supermarkets is currently small and, although their presence and power will inevitably grow, just 23% of the surveyed households obtain some of their food from supermarkets and only 3% had been to one in the week prior to the survey. Over three-quarters of the households never shop at supermarkets.

TABLE 11: Household Food Sources				
	Region	Maputo		
	% Using Source	% Using Source	% Using Source Weekly	% Used Source in Previous Week
Market sources				
Supermarket	79	23	8	3
Informal market/street food	70	98	92	94
Small food outlet	68	77	22	40
Non-market sources				
Grow it	22	22	12	15
Share meals with other households	21	19	7	11
Borrow food	21	12	8	8
Food provided by other households	20	10	3	6
Food remittances	8	12	0	6
Food transfers from rural areas	28	8	0	–
Charitable sources				
Community food kitchen	4	<1	0	<1
Food aid	2	1	0	1

Small shops (including independent grocers, butcheries and bakeries) are regularly patronized by 77% of the households and 40% had obtained food there in the previous week. The most common type of small retail outlet is the *loja*, which is owned and operated by local licensed retailers and carries a wide variety of consumer and household goods as well as fresh produce.[33] In terms of food stocks, *lojas* specialize in non-perishables including canned goods and frozen fish and poultry. In many cities, small outlets are the first to feel the pressure from supermarket expansion, but in Maputo, where the informal food economy is by far the most important source of food, this will probably take some time. Almost all the households regularly obtain food from informal sellers and over 90% do so at least once a week, many on a daily basis. For many households, daily purchasing is necessitated by unpredictable daily incomes and a lack of accumulated funds.[34] Such "fragmentary purchasing" raises the unit cost per item and leads to higher household expenditures on food.

Non-market sources of food proved to be far less important to the surveyed households. Urban agriculture, for example, is consistently advocated by international agencies as a viable solution to urban food insecurity. One advocate of urban agriculture in Mozambique has noted that "the development of the agricultural use of the urban and peri-urban land can be a solution not only to enhance food security of the urban poor, but also to ameliorate their self-esteem and hence give them dignity."[35] Another study claims that in late colonial and early post-colonial Maputo, "the vast majority of urban women continued their familiar rural agricultural work, wielding their hoes and wrapping themselves in their printed cotton *capulanas* in a new setting."[36] As a result, women's agriculture supposedly "profoundly shaped" the character of urbanization in Mozambique. In the 1990s, however, increasing numbers of women turned to working in the informal economy and urban agriculture began to decline in significance. In 2008, less than a quarter (22%) of the surveyed households produced any of their own food and only 15% had consumed home-grown produce in the week prior to the survey. As in other cities in the region, the role of urban agriculture in poor urban communities is easily exaggerated.[37]

Various forms of informal social protection are relied on by a minority of households, but less so than in the region as a whole. For example, sharing meals with other households is close to the regional average (19% versus 21%) but obtaining food from other households or borrowing food is less common (10-12% compared to 20-21%). Regular use of these sources is even less common, suggesting that these sources are only called upon in times of crisis. One recent study suggested that these coping mechanisms are in decline and that households are less willing or able to share

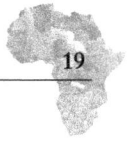

with anyone outside the household: "The dissolution of these safety nets … points to a nuclearization of economic decisions which include food access strategies." As a result, "the household comes to be the primary mediator of social coping and food access without the support or involvement of relatives and neighbours who were previously deemed crucial to these activities."[38]

Households that have migrant members in South Africa do receive food remittances but not regularly. AFSUN surveys in other cities have demonstrated that informal rural-urban transfers of food outside market channels are a significant source of food for poor urban households that maintain strong links with the countryside.[39] However, while 23% of households had received food from outside Maputo in the previous year, only 9% had received food directly from the countryside. Most of these transfers occur only a few times a year and consist primarily of cereals, fruit and vegetables. A study of six smaller urban centres in Mozambique suggests that rural-urban links are much stronger there and that there is a "constant interchange of remittances and goods from urbanites and food items from (rural) family members when crops are good."[40] However, while this seems logical as many of these centres have large agricultural hinterlands, the actual evidence presented is slight.

6. LEVELS OF FOOD INSECURITY

AFSUN uses four international cross-cultural scales developed by the Food and Nutrition Technical Assistance Project (FANTA) to assess levels of food insecurity:

- Household Food Insecurity Access Scale (HFIAS): The HFIAS measures the degree of food insecurity during the month prior to the survey.[41] An HFIAS score is calculated for each household based on answers to nine "frequency-of-occurrence" questions. The minimum score is 0 and the maximum is 27. The higher the score, the more food insecurity the household experienced. The individual questions also provide insights into the nature of food insecurity experienced.

- Household Food Insecurity Access Prevalence Indicator (HFIAP): The HFIAP indicator uses the responses to the HFIAS questions to group households into four levels of household food insecurity: food secure, mildly food insecure, moderately food insecure and severely food insecure.[42]

- Household Dietary Diversity Scale (HDDS): Dietary diversity refers to how many food groups are consumed within the household in the previous 24 hours.[43] The maximum number, based on the FAO classification of food groups for Africa, is 12. An increase in the average number of different food groups consumed provides a quantifiable measure of improved household food access.

- Months of Adequate Household Food Provisioning Indicator (MAHFP): The MAHFP indicator captures changes in the household's ability to ensure that food is available above a minimum level the year round.[44] Households are asked to identify in which months (during the past 12) they did not have access to sufficient food to meet their household needs.

The HFIAS score for the surveyed households is 10.4, which is very close to the average for the region as a whole (10.3) (Table 12). Maputo's poor would also appear to be less food insecure than those in most other cities surveyed including the South African cities of Cape Town (10.7) and Msunduzi (11.3). Only Windhoek, Blantyre and Johannesburg had better scores than Maputo.

TABLE 12: Maputo HFIAS Scores Compared to Other Cities

	Mean	Median	No.
Manzini, Swaziland	14.9	14.7	489
Harare, Zimbabwe	14.7	16.0	454
Maseru, Lesotho	12.8	13.0	795
Lusaka, Zambia	11.5	11.0	386
Msunduzi, South Africa	11.3	11.0	548
Gaborone, Botswana	10.8	11.0	391
Cape Town, South Africa	10.7	11.0	1,026
Maputo, Mozambique	10.4	10.0	389
Windhoek, Namibia	9.3	9.0	436
Blantyre, Malawi	5.3	3.7	431
Johannesburg, South Africa	4.7	1.5	976
Region	10.3	10	6,327

However, a different picture emerges when the HFIAP is used to divide the Maputo households into four food security categories (Table 13). First, Maputo has one of the lowest proportions of severely food insecure households in the region (54%, when in most other cities the proportion is 60-80%). However, this positive finding should not detract from the fact that just over half of the households in Maputo experience constant food insecurity. Second, only 5% of the households were found to be completely food secure (well below the regional average of 15%), which is one of the worst scores in the region (only Harare and Lusaka had a lower figure). Third, Maputo has the highest proportion of moderately food

insecure households in the region (at 32%, considerably higher than the regional average of 20%). These figures all suggest that Maputo has two basic kinds of household: half with severe food insecurity and the other half in a state of chronic food insecurity.

TABLE 13: Maputo HFIAP Scores Compared to Other Cities				
	Food Secure %	Mildly Food Insecure %	Moderately Food Insecure %	Severely Food Insecure %
Harare, Zimbabwe	2	3	24	72
Lusaka, Zambia	4	3	24	69
Maseru, Lesotho	5	6	25	65
Maputo, Mozambique	5	9	32	54
Manzini, Swaziland	6	3	13	79
Msunduzi, South Africa	7	6	27	60
Gaborone, Botswana	12	6	19	63
Cape Town, South Africa	15	5	12	68
Windhoek, Namibia	18	5	14	63
Blantyre, Malawi	34	15	30	21
Johannesburg, South Africa	44	14	15	27
Region	16	7	20	57

To better understand what aspects of food insecurity most affect Maputo households, we disaggregated the answers to the individual HFIAS questions. As Table 14 shows, 56% of household heads sometimes or often worried that the household would not have enough food to eat. And these worries seem justified for the 45-50% that had sometimes or often responded by eating smaller meals or fewer meals in a day. There is also a group of extremely insecure households that sometimes/often have no food at all (21%), in which household members go to sleep hungry (16%) and go a whole day and night without eating (10%). But the majority do not experience such critical shortages of food. Rather, it is the quality of what they eat that is their major concern.

The Maputo diet is dominated by the consumption of rice and bread.[45] Rice has rapidly become more important than maize as a staple.[46] Consumption of fresh and frozen fish is relatively common, although much of the frozen fish is imported from Angola. Chicken is the most common other form of animal protein and beef is rarely eaten. A fairly wide variety of vegetables (including beans, squash, onions, cassava and cabbage) is consumed but not in great quantities. The only fruits to feature in the average diet are coconuts and tomatoes. This might lead us to the conclusion that the diet of the Maputo poor is relatively diverse. In fact, the answers of surveyed households to the HFIAS questions indicate that around 60% had not been able to eat the kinds of food they preferred and 52% had eaten foods that they did not want to because of a lack of resources to purchase the desired diet. In addition, nearly 60% noted that their diet was limited in variety for the same reason. The HDDS quantifies this more precisely (Figure 7). The average surveyed household scored 5.67 out of 12. Nearly half of the households (47%) had a score of 5 or lower. Comparatively, this puts Maputo in a better place than cities such as Harare, Lusaka and Msunduzi but worse than cities such as Johannesburg, Cape Town, Blantyre and Windhoek.

TABLE 14: Responses to Food Insecurity	
In the last month, did you:	% Sometimes/ Often
Worry that your household would not have enough food?	55.8
Not eat the kinds of foods you preferred because of a lack of resources?	62.2
Eat a limited variety of foods due to a lack of resources?	58.5
Eat foods you did not want to because of a lack of resources to obtain other types of food?	51.6
Eat smaller meals than you needed because there was not enough food?	46.7
Eat fewer meals in a day because there was not enough food?	45.0
Eat no food of any kind because of a lack of resources to obtain food?	20.9
Go to sleep hungry because there was not enough food?	16.5
Go a whole day and night without eating anything?	9.6

FIGURE 7: Regional HDDS Scores

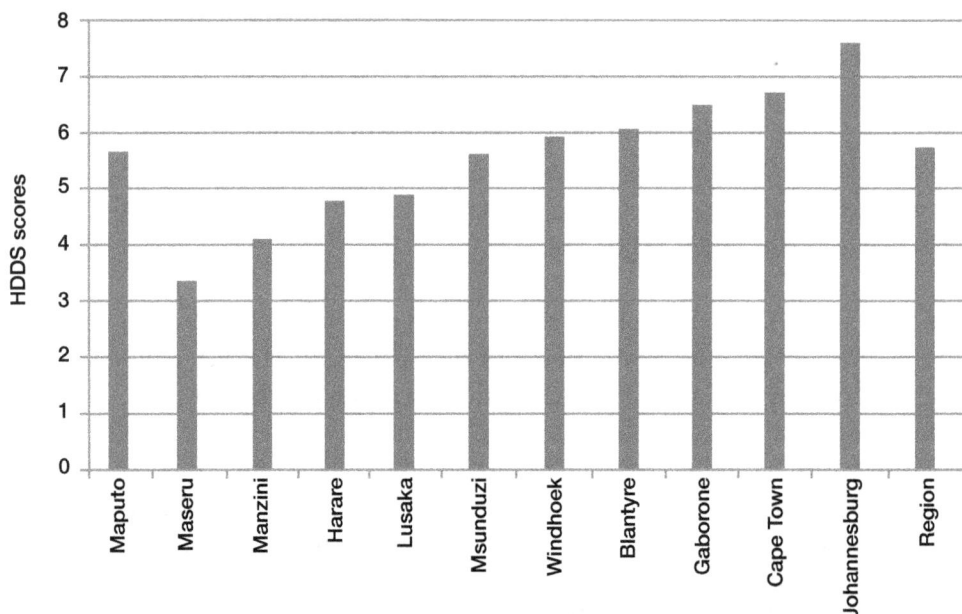

The fourth FANTA indicator is the MAHFP, which shows whether there are fluctuations in levels of food insecurity throughout the year. The mean household MAHFP was 8.32, which indicates nearly 4 months of inadequate food provisioning during the year (Figure 8).

FIGURE 8: Distribution of MAHFP Scores in Maputo

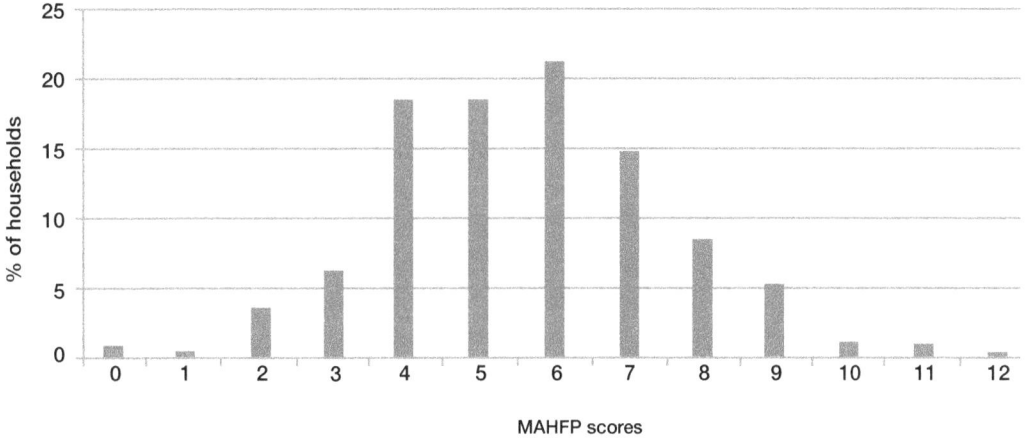

An analysis of the MAHFP shows that the hungriest months (when 35-40% of households have inadequate provisioning) occur from August to November (Figure 9). December is the least food-insecure month overall.

FIGURE 9: Proportion of Households with Inadequate Food Provisioning by Month

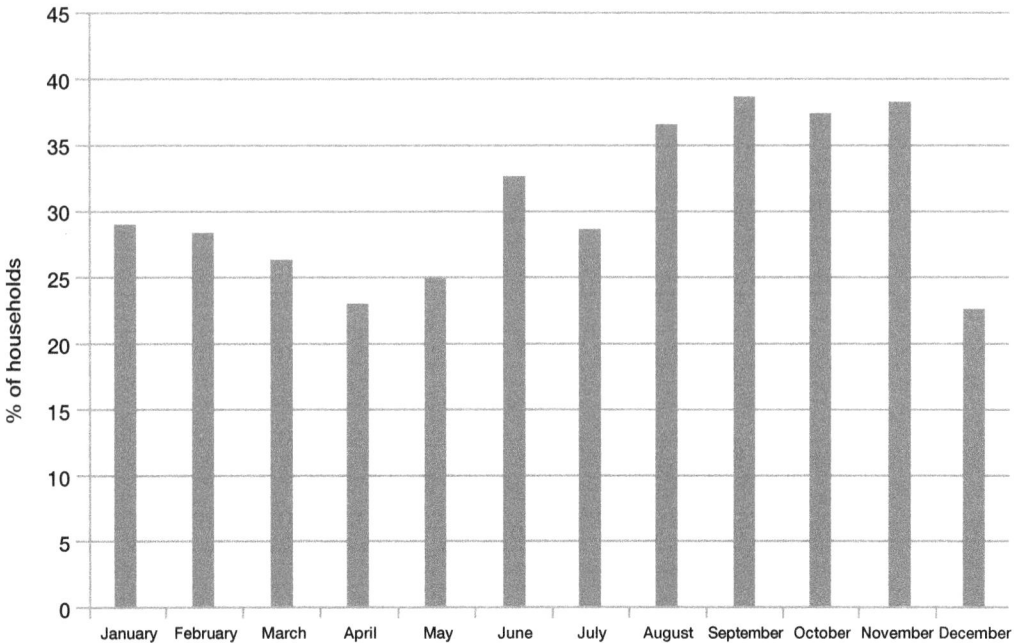

7. DETERMINANTS OF VARIABILITY IN HOUSEHOLD FOOD SECURITY

A number of demographic variables were cross-tabulated with means scores for three of the food security measures discussed above (HFIAS, HDDS and MAHFP) (Table 15). The primary objective was to identify inter-household differences in vulnerability. First, there is a clear relationship between household size and food insecurity scores on two of the indicators: the HFIAS and the MAHFP. As household size increases, so does food insecurity as measured by the HFIAS (from 10.27 amongst households with 1-5 members to 11.07 for those with more than 10 members). Similarly, the MAHFP consistently falls with increasing household size (indicating a greater number of months with inadequate food provisioning as size increases). The only anomaly is with the HDDS. Households with 1-5 members have lower dietary diversity (5.72) than those with more than 10 members (5.81). The lowest HDDS score is in the group of households with 6 to 10 members. While we might expect the smaller households to have more dietary diversity than mid-sized households, it is not immediately clear why the largest households have the most diverse diets.

TABLE 15: Variations in Mean Food Insecurity Scores			
Household size	HFIAS	HDDS	MAHFP
1–5	10.27	5.72	9.66
6–10	10.30	5.60	9.44
>10	11.07	5.81	9.09
Household type	HFIAS	HDDS	MAHFP
Female-centred	10.84	5.36	9.04
Male-centred	9.80	5.81	10.26
Nuclear	9.79	5.50	9.59
Extended	10.47	5.91	9.54
Income tercile	HFIAS	HDDS	MAHFP
Lowest	13.22	5.07	8.46
Middle	10.73	5.67	9.54
Highest	7.74	6.14	10.21
LPI score	HFIAS	HDDS	MAHFP
0.00–1.00	7.12	6.24	10.29
1.01–2.00	12.69	5.32	8.97
2.01–3.00	17.13	4.50	7.31

Second, in terms of the relationship between household type and food insecurity, it is clear that female-centred households are the worst off. They have the highest levels of food insecurity (HFIAS of 10.84), the lowest dietary diversity (HDDS 5.36) and the fewest number of months of adequate food provisioning (MAHP 9.04). Extended households are next in terms of levels of food insecurity (HFIAS 10.47 and MAHFP 9.54). However, consistent with the finding above that dietary diversity is greatest in the larger households, the extended households have the best HDDS scores of any household type. Male-centred and nuclear families have almost identical HFIAS scores but the former clearly have the fewest number of months of inadequate food provisioning (less than 2 months).

Third, food security is strongly correlated with household income. Households in the lowest income tercile have an extremely high HFIAS of 13.2, compared with only 7.7 for those in the highest income tercile. They also have the lowest dietary diversity score (5.1 compared with 6.1 for those in the highest income tercile). Finally, they have a significantly greater number of months of inadequate provisioning, with an MAHFP score of 8.5 (compared with 10.2 for the highest income tercile). These households therefore report an inadequate food supply for three and a half months per year compared with less than 2 for better-off households. However, it also needs stressing that in absolute terms even the latter are far from being food secure.

Fourth, the poorest households (as measured by the LPI) are also the most food insecure. Table 15 divides the household LPI scores into three groups and cross-tabulates with the three food security measures. The HFIAS scores range from 7.1 (for the least poor group) to 17.1 (for the most poor). Dietary diversity scores are 6.2 for the least poor and 4.5 for the poorest. Finally, the MAHFP index varies from 9.0 for the least poor to 6.64 for the poorest. These differences, even within generally poor neighbour-hoods, are highly significant statistically and testify both to the rigour of the LPI and internal differentiation in poverty and related food insecurity.

8. Conclusion

February 2008 saw widespread rioting on the streets of Maputo. With minivan taxis (or *chapas*) the first to be attacked by protestors, some blamed the riots on the rising costs of transport.[47] Subsequent analyses have re-labelled them "food riots" and part of a general global protest movement that shook the streets of many cities across the Global South in the wake of escalating food prices on international, regional and local markets.[48] Whether or not increased food prices were the direct cause of the protests, it is clear from the AFSUN survey that poor households throughout Maputo were severely impacted by food price escalation in 2008. If there is some dispute about whether the 2008 unrest was "transport riots" or "food riots", no such ambiguity surrounds a second wave of protests in September 2010. The protests followed an announcement that the government was withdrawing its subsidy on imported wheat and that, as a result, the price of a loaf of bread would immediately increase by 25%. The announcement coincided with sharp increases in the cost of other basic needs such as water and fuel. Following several days of rioting, in which a number of people died, the government reversed its position and maintained the subsidy. One study of participation in the riots notes that no group in the poor areas of the city absented themselves from taking part.[49] Given the high levels of food insecurity documented in this report, the high proportion of meagre household income that is spent on food purchase and the reliance on a small number of staples (including bread) in the daily diet, broad reaction to sudden food price increases is hardly surprising.

The danger of focusing only on episodic violent protest is that it might imply that there is no cause for concern during intervening periods of quiescence. On the contrary, as this report clearly demonstrates, food insecurity is a fact of life for the vast majority of households across Maputo's poverty belt. Households exist in a constant state of food insecurity manifested in a lack of access to sufficient affordable food, poor dietary quality and undernutrition. Household income is meagre and only those households with access to wage income have any chance of holding food insecurity at bay. The most food secure households are those with higher household incomes. Households purchase the vast majority of the food they consume and spend half of their income on food. With a vibrant and dynamic informal food economy, Maputo's poor are surrounded by fresh and processed food. Food availability is therefore not the primary determinant of food insecurity in Maputo. Certainly large-scale food import from South Africa and further afield makes the market price of food inherently volatile. But prices for the consumer are also driven down by the fact that there is intense competition among vendors on the streets and in the marketplaces. The real cause of food insecurity (manifested in high HFIAS scores and low HDDS and MAHFP scores) is high urban unemployment and a lack of regular and decent-paying work.

The food protests in Maputo had the effect of intensifying policy debate around three key issues: food imports and domestic food production, food pricing, and social protection.[50] First, the rapid growth of food imports of grains since 2000 has come under intense scrutiny since reliance on

importation makes the country more vulnerable to international price fluctuations. For example, imports of wheat increased by 600% between 2000 and 2006.[51] On the other hand, imports are often far cheaper than local produce (a fact that explains why Brazilian frozen chicken is commonplace in Maputo's markets). International agencies and donors have pushed the conventional wisdom that increased local agricultural production will by definition mean cheaper and more accessible food for Mozambican consumers.[52] The 2010 WFP/FAO Comprehensive Africa Agricultural Development Plan, the 2008 Plan of Action for Agriculture, and the 2011 Strategic Plan for Agricultural Development are meant to operationalize a "green revolution" in Mozambique that would supposedly see reduced reliance on food imports, expanded output, the incorporation of smallholders into agricultural value-chains, poverty reduction and cheaper food.[53]

The second response has been intensified debate about food price policy and whether continuing food subsidies by government are affordable and necessary.[54] The Mozambican government has been under strong pressure from neo-liberal international financial institutions and Western donors to remove its extensive subsidies on staples such as rice, wheat and maize. In 2009, in response to the global food price crisis, the government reduced its import tariffs on rice, wheat and maize from 25% to 2.5%. The cost of its existing food and fuel subsidies soared by over 900% in 2009, increasing fiscal pressures to reduce or eliminate subsidies.[55] The outrage on the streets of Maputo quickly led to a reversal of this position. Debate continued on food subsidies after the violence subsided, with one commentator showing that subsidies in Mozambique clearly and disproportionately benefit those in higher income groups.[56] This has led to suggestions that universal subsidies should be replaced by subsidies targeted at the poorest and most insecure. In 2011, for example, the Mozambican Parliament debated a proposal for a food-basket subsidy targeted at very low income households. Opinions divided on whether this should be an ongoing programme or whether it should only be invoked during emergencies (such as sharp and uncontrollable food price spikes).

Third, debate about state-funded social protection has intensified. The AFSUN survey shows that informal social support mechanisms are not particularly strong in Maputo, which means that there is an even stronger case for formalized social protection. As one recent report concluded, existing social protection schemes "have limited coverage, offer fragmented assistance and are not well resourced."[57] The Food Subsidy Programme, the main protection programme created by legal provision in 1993, was one-third donor funded in 2009.[58] In 2008, there were 143,000 beneficiary households containing 287,000 individuals receiving MZN110-300

per month. The main target was the elderly but fewer than 20% of house-holds with elderly people were being reached. The Direct Social Support Programme was designed to provide material support (including food) to destitute households. In 2008, it covered 24,000 households nationally. How many of these beneficiary households were in Maputo is unclear.[59]

Recent attempts to give effect to the legislation and to develop and resource a more systematic approach to social protection are embodied in the Multi-Sectoral Action Plan for the Reduction of Chronic Undernu-trition.[60] The Plan identifies one of the key manifestations of food inse-curity in Mozambique – child undernutrition – and identifies a set of existing and planned social protection measures at the national level. The Plan contains strategic objectives relevant to urban populations including: (a) activities with impact on the nutritional status of adolescents; (b) inter-ventions with impact on the health and nutrition of women of reproduc-tive age; (c) nutrition activities for children in the first two years of life; (d) household-oriented activities to improve access and utilization of foods with high nutritional value; (d) human resource capacity development in nutrition and (e) provision of disagreggated data on food and nutri-tion security in the country.[61] The most relevant interventions for urban populations include nutrition education and promotion of the consump-tion of foods with high nutritional value, micronutrient supplementation programmes, school feeding programmes (which currently cover only 10% of school-age children nationwide), school gardens, the Food Sub-sidy Programme (which distributed food to 140,000 destitute households in 2009 but less than 1% were in Maputo) and food support for Orphans and Vulnerable Children (OVCs).

In 2010, the National Strategy for Basic Social Security (ENSSB) defined four areas for future intervention: (a) direct social action (such as cash and in-kind transfers), (b) health social action (such as promotion of access to basic healthcare), (c) productive social action (such as public works and microfinance) and (d) education social action.[62] In 2012, four main social protection programmes were underway: (a) the Basic Social Subsidy Pro-gramme (PSSB), which replaces the Food Subsidy Programme and is aimed at households with no other means of support; (b) the Direct Social Support Programme (PASD) to support vulnerable households facing shocks that cannot be overcome by their own means; (c) the Social Wel-fare Social Services Programme (PSSAS); and (d) the Productive Social Welfare Programme. The budget for the social protection programmes was USD37 million, a 25% increase from 2011. Exactly what kinds of transfers are envisaged is not clear but a basic universal or targeted child grant would be a highly desirable intervention to mitigate severe food insecurity in the urban environment where, as this report demonstrates,

households are forced to purchase virtually all of their food. In the longer term, only inclusive economic growth with more and decent employment is likely to ameliorate food insecurity significantly in Maputo but, in the interim, a more effective social protection system is highly desirable.

In conclusion, several concrete recommendations can be made to take the findings of this report further:

- This report is the first systematic study of *urban* food insecurity in a country that is predominantly or exclusively seen as suffering chronic rural food insecurity. Urban food insecurity, not just in Maputo but more generally, needs to be placed higher on the national and municipal policy agenda, given the rapid rate of urbanization and the country's increasingly urban future. This issue should not only be addressed during and after food riots but be incorporated systematically into all development planning.

- The report provides a cross-sectional picture of the severity of food insecurity in Maputo in 2008. A follow-up survey is urgently recommended to provide up-to-date information and a longitudinal picture of food security trends and determinants in the city at the household level in the city's poverty belt.

- The establishment of an urban food security observatory for Mozambique is recommended to collect data and monitor food insecurity on an ongoing basis, to provide a systematic basis for sound and workable policy interventions and to evaluate the impact of those interventions.

- The city of Maputo urgently needs its own food security strategy – one that is multi-sectoral and policy-oriented and based on a better understanding of food flows into and within the city, the operation of the city's informal food economy and the likely impacts of formal retailing for the food security of the urban poor.

ENDNOTES

1   J. Crush and B. Frayne, *The Invisible Crisis: Urban Food Security in Southern Africa*. AFSUN Urban Food Security Series No. 1, Cape Town, 2010, p. 24.

2   UN-HABITAT, *The State of African Cities 2008: A Framework for Addressing Urban Challenges in Africa* (Nairobi, 2008).

3   Ibid., p. 23.

4   M. Paulo, C. Rosário and I. Tvedten, *'Xiculungo': Social Relations of Urban Poverty in Maputo, Mozambique* (Bergen: Chr Michelsen Institute), p. 17.

5   World Bank, *Mozambique – Second Maputo Municipal Development Program Project*. Washington, DC: World Bank (2010).

6   P. Jenkins, "Maputo" *Cities* 17 (2000): 207-218.

7   C. Kihato, L. Royston, J. Raimundo and I. Raimundo, "Multiple Land Regimes: Rethinking Land Governance in Maputo's Peri-Urban Spaces" *Urban Forum* 24(2013), p. 70.

8   C. Barros, A. Chivangue and A. Samagaio, "Urban Dynamics in Maputo, Mozambique" *Cities* 36 (2014): 74-82.

9   Ibid., p. 80.

10   Paulo et al., *'Xiculungo'* p. 29.

11   Ibid., p. 56.

12   Ibid., pp. 59-64.

13   Ibid., p. 63.

14   Ibid., pp. 63-4.

15   Ibid.; B. Byiers, "Informality in Mozambique: Characteristics, Performance and Policy Issues" Report for USAID, Washington DC, 2008; N. Matsinhe, D. Juízo, B. Macheve and C. dos Santos, "Regulation of Formal and Informal Water Service Providers in Peri-Urban Areas of Maputo, Mozambique" *Physics and Chemistry of the Earth* 33 (2008): 841-9; B. Byiers, "Enterprise Survey Evidence" In C. Arndt and F. Tarp (Eds.), *Taxation in a Low-Income Economy: The Case of Mozambique* (New York: Routledge, 2009). C. Allen and E. Jossias, "Mapping of the Policy Context and *Catadores* Organizations in Maputo, Mozambique" WIEGO Organizing Brief No. 6, Cambridge MA, 2011; M. Paulo, C. Rosário and I. Tvedten, 'Xiculungo' Revisited: Assessing the Implications of PARPA 11 in Maputo 2007-2010 (Bergen: Chr. Michelsen Institute, 2011); I. Raimundo and J. Raimundo, "Operation of the Market Study Land Access in Urban Areas: The Case of Maputo" Report for Urban LandMark, Pretoria, 2012; G. Carolini. "Framing Water, Sanitation, and Hygiene Needs Among Female-Headed Households in Periurban Maputo, Mozambique" *American Journal of Public Health* 102(2012): 256-261; Kihato et al, "Multiple Land Regimes"; V. Zuin, L. Ortolano and J. Davis, "The Entrepreneurship Myth in Small-Scale Service Provision: Water Resale in Maputo, Mozambique" *Journal of Water, Sanitation and Hygiene for Development* (in press).

16   A. Prista, J. Maia, A. Damasceno and G. Beunen, "Anthropometric Indicators of Nutritional Status: Implications for Fitness, Activity, and Health in School-Age Children and Adolescents from Maputo, Mozambique" *American Journal of Clinical Nutrition* 77 (2003): 952-9.

17   F. de Vletter, "Migration and Development in Mozambique: Poverty, Inequality and Survival" *Development Southern Africa* 24 (2007): 137-53; I. Raimundo, "International Migration Management and Development in Mozambique: What Strategies?" *International Migration* 47 (2009): 93-122.

18   D. Vidal, "Living In, Out Of, and Between Two Cities: Migrants from Maputo in Johannesburg" *Urban Forum* 21 (2010): 55-68; R. Muanamoha, B. Maharaj and E. Preston-Whyte, "Social Networks and Undocumented Mozambican Migration to South Africa" *Geoforum* 41 (2010): 885-96; J. Galleho and M. Mendola, "Labour Migration and Social Networks Participation in Southern Mozambique" *Economica* 80(2013): 721-59.

19   Ministry of Planning and Development (MPD), *Poverty and Well-Being in Mozambique: Third National Poverty Assessment* (Maputo, 2010).

20   Ibid., p. xi.

21   The Mozambique currency is the New Metical (MZN). Currency values and conversion to USD is based on exchange rates at the time of the survey in 2008 (USD1 = MZN24).

22   Afrobarometer, "Lived Poverty in Africa: Desperation, Hope and Patience" Briefing Paper No. 11, Cape Town, 2004. The LPI is based on answers to questions about how often a household has gone without certain basic household items in the previous year (food, medical attention, cooking fuel and a cash income). Respondents answer on a five-point scale: never; just once or twice; several times; many times; always. A mean LPI score is then computed for each item: a mean score closer to 0 indicates fewer households 'going without' and a score closer to 4 indicates more households 'going without'.

23   V. Agadjanian, "'Men Doing 'Women's Work': Masculinity and Gender Relations Among Street Vendors in Maputo, Mozambique" In L. Ouzgane and R. Morrell (Eds.), *African Masculinities* (Pietermaritzburg: UKZN Press, 2005), pp. 247-59; A. Brooks, "Riches from Rags or Persistent Poverty? The Working Lives of Secondhand Clothing Vendors in Maputo, Mozambique" *Textile: The Journal of Cloth and Culture* 10 (2010): 222-37; R. Brouwer, "Mobile Phones in Mozambique: The Street Trade in Airtime in Maputo City" *Science, Technology and Society* 15(2010): 135-54; A. Ulset, "Formalization of Informal Marketplaces: A Case Study of the Xikhelene Market, Maputo, Mozambique" M.A. Thesis, University of Oslo, 2010, pp. 66-83; R. Albers, V. Güida, M. Rusca and K. Schwartz, "Unleashing Entrepreneurs or Controlling Unruly Providers? The Formalisation of Small-Scale Water Providers in Greater Maputo, Mozambique" *Journal of Development Studies* 49 (2013): 470-82.,

24   J. Crush and B. Frayne, *Pathways to Insecurity: Urban Food Supply and Access in Southern African Cities*. AFSUN Urban Food Security Series No. 3, Cape Town, 2010, p. 31.

25   Agadjanian, "'Men Doing Women's Work'" p. 259.

26   Ulset, "Formalization of Informal Marketplaces" pp. 68-9.

27   Ibid., p. 72.

28   Ibid., pp. 73-4.

29   Ibid., pp. 90-6.

30   S. Stein, "Urban Foodscapes: Urban Food Security and Everyday Lives in an Informal Settlement of Maputo, Mozambique" M. Phil. Thesis, Oxford University, 2012, pp. 82-3.

31   J. Crush & B. Frayne, "Supermarket Expansion and the Informal Food Economy of Southern African Cities: Implications for Urban Food Security" *Journal of Southern African Studies* 37(2011): 781-807; E. Dakor, "Exploring the Fourth Wave of Supermarket Evolution: Concepts of Value and Complexity in Africa" *International Journal of Managing Value and Supply Chains* 3(2012): 25-37.

32   D. Miller, "'Spaces of Resistance': African Workers at Shoprite in Maputo and Lusaka" *Africa Development* 31(2006): 27-49.

33   Stein, "Urban Foodscapes", p. 59.

34   Ibid., p. 75.

35   I. Madaleno, "Alleviating Poverty in Maputo, Mozambique" at http://www.cityfarmer.org/mozambique.html

36   K. Sheldon, "Markets and Gardens: Placing Women in the History of Urban Mozambique" *Canadian Journal of African Studies* 37 (2003): 358-95.

37   J. Crush, A. Hovorka and D. Tevera, "Food Security in Southern African Cities: The Place of Urban Agriculture" *Progress in Development Studies* 11 (2011): 285-305.

38   Stein, "Urban Foodscapes", p. 82.

39   B. Frayne, "Pathways of Food: Mobility and Food Transfer in Southern African Cities" *International Development Planning Review* 32 (2010): 83-104.

40   J. Dávila, E. Kyrou, T. Nunez and J. Sumich, "Urbanisation and Municipal Development in Mozambique: Urban Poverty and Rural-Urban Linkages" Development Planning Unit, University College London, 2008.

41   J. Coates, A. Swindale and P. Bilinsky, "Household Food Insecurity Access Scale (HFIAS) for Measurement of Food Access: Indicator Guide (Version 3)" Food and Nutrition Technical Assistance Project, Academy for Educational Development, Washington DC, 2007.

42   Ibid.

43   A. Swindale and P. Bilinsky, "Household Dietary Diversity Score (HDDS) for Measurement of Household Food Access: Indicator Guide (Version 2)" Food and Nutrition Technical Assistance Project, Academy for Educational Development, Washington DC, 2006.

44   P. Bilinsky and A. Swindale, "Months of Adequate Household Food Provisioning (MAHFP) for Measurement of Household Food Access: Indicator Guide" Food and Nutrition Technical Assistance Project, Academy for Educational Development, Washington DC, 2007.

45   National Directorate of Studies and Policy Analysis, *Poverty and Wellbeing in Mozambique*, p. 131.

46   Rice consumption in Mozambique increased dramatically after 2000. National consumption of rice more than doubled from 8kg/person/year in 2000 to 21kg/person/year in 2007. Mozambique's total milled rice production in 2009 was about 157,000 metric tons. Estimated total rice consumption is 550,000 tons with annual average import of 350,000 tons; IFPRI, "Rice in Mozambique" at http://www.irri.org/index.php?option=com_k2&view=item&id=11561:rice-in-mozambique&lang=en

47   J. Sumich, "Nationalism, Urban Poverty and Identity in Maputo, Mozambique" Working Paper No. 68, Crisis States Research Centre, LSE, London, 2010, p. 5.

48   J. Hanlon, "Mozambique: The Panic and Rage of the Poor" *Review of African Political Economy* 36(2009): 125-30; J. Berazneva and D. Lee, "Explaining the African Food Riots of 2007-1008: An Empirical Analysis" *Food Policy* 39(2013): 28-39.

49   B. Bertelsen, "Effervescence and Ephemerality: Dynamics of Urban Rioting and State Sovereignty in Mozambique" Presentation at African Studies Workshop, Harvard University, 2013.

50   C. Arndt, R. Benfica, N. Maximiano, A. Nucifora and J. Thurlow, "Higher Fuel and Food Prices: Impacts and Responses for Mozambique" *Agricultural Economics* 39(2008): 497-511.

51   V. Nhate, C. Massingarela and V. Salvucci, "The Political Economy of Food Price Policy: Country Case Study of Mozambique" WIDER Working Paper No. 2013/037, United Nations University, 2013, p. 3.

52   J. Thurlow, "Agricultural Growth Options for Poverty Reduction in

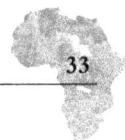

Mozambique: Preliminary Report Prepared for Mozambique's Ministry of Agriculture and Strategic Analysis and Knowledge Support System (SAKSS)" International Food Policy Research Institute, Washington DC, 2008; FAO/WFP, "Special Report: Crop and Food Security Assessment Mission to Mozambique" Rome, 2010.

53   Government of Mozambique, "Strategic Plan for Agricultural Development. PEDSA 2010-2019" Ministry of Agriculture, Maputo, 2010; B. Cunguara and J. Garrett, "Agricultural Sector in Mozambique: Situation Analysis, Constraints and Opportunities for Agricultural Growth" Report for Dialogue on Promotion of Agricultural Growth in Mozambique Workshop, Maputo, 2011; K. Pauw, J. Thurlow, R. Uaiene and J. Mazunda, "Agricultural Growth and Poverty Reduction in Mozambique: Technical Analysis in Support of the Comprehensive Agriculture Development Program (CAADP)" Working Paper No. 2, Mozambique Strategy Support Program, IFPRI, Washington DC, 2012. For more critical assessments see T. Jayne, D. Mather and E. Mghenyi, "Principal Challenges Confronting Smallholder Agriculture in Sub-Saharan Africa" *World Development* 38(2010): 1384-98; B. Cuangara and I. Darnhofer, "Assessing the Impact of Improved Agricultural Technologies on Household Income in Rural Mozambique" *Food Policy* 36(2011): 378-90; K. Kajisa and E. Payongayong, "Potential of and Constraints to the Rice Green Revolution in Mozambique: A Case Study of the Chokwe Irrigation Scheme" *Food Policy* 36(2011): 615-26.

54   Nhate et al. "Political Economy of Food Price Policy."

55   B. Shane, "A Cacophony of Policy Responses: Evidence from Fourteen Countries During the 2007/08 Food Price Crisis" WIDER Working Paper No. 2013/029, United Nations University, 2013, p. 9.

56   A. Nucifora, "On the Riots in Mozambique: Are Subsidies the Solution?" at http://blogs.worldbank.org/africacan/on-the-riots-in-mozambique-are-subsidies-the-solution

57   AfDB, OECD, UNDP and UNECA, *African Economic Outlook* 2012: Mozambique, p. 12.

58   Law 4/2007 of 7 February (Law on Social Protection) and Decree 85/2009 of 29 December (approving the Regulations for the Basic Social Security Subsystem) lay the foundations for a three-tier social protection system in Mozambique: (a) basic social security, (b) mandatory social security and (c) complementary social security; see Republic of Mozambique, *National Basic Social Security Strategy 2010-2014*, Ministry of Women and Social Action, Maputo, 2010, Section 1.3.1.

59   An impact evaluation of the Basic Food Subsidy Programme in 2008 reported food security improvements but only sampled rural recipients: F. Soares and C. Teixeira, "Impact Evaluation of the Food Subsidy Programme in Mozambique" Policy Brief No. 17, International Policy Centre for Inclusive Growth, 2010; K. Silvester, L. Fidalgo and N. Taimo, "Transforming Cash Transfers: Beneficiary and Community Perspectives on the Basic Social Subsidy Programme in Mozambique" Overseas Development Institute, London, 2012.

60   Republic of Mozambique, *Multi-Sectoral Action Plan for the Reduction of Chronic Undernutrition 2011-2015 (2020)* Maputo, 2010.

61   Ibid., pp. 37-8.

62   Republic of Mozambique, *National Basic Social Security Strategy 2010-2014*.